WALKS FROM YOUR

Ullswater & Haweswater

by
Tom Bowker

Dalesman
1992

Key to maps

GREY TARN / GREY GILL	tarn and beck
ULLSWATER	lake
═══════	road or walled lane
🌲🌲🌲🌲	woodland
--→---→---	footpath with direction arrow
▪	building
—)(—	bridge
∞∞∞∞∞∞∞∞	wall that is particularly useful for navigation
‖‖‖‖‖‖‖‖	fence that is particularly useful for navigation
•	points of interest; cairns, caves, car-parks
▲ PLACE FELL	summit
⋀	campsite
⌢⌢⌢⌢	quarry, crag, or craggy fellside

Contents

Cover map by Barbara Yates.
Sketch maps by Helen Bowker.

The Dalesman Publishing Company Ltd.,
Clapham, via Lancaster, LA2 8EB

First published 1987
Second edition 1989
Third edition 1992
© Tom Bowker, 1987, 1992

ISBN: 1 85568 038 6

Printed by Peter Fretwell & Sons Ltd., Keighley, West Yorkshire.

INTRODUCTION

THIS guidebook is not for the motorist who is looking for a couple of miles' stroll in his driving shoes. Nor is it for the hardened long-distance fellwalker. It is written principally for the motorist-cum-walker who is prepared to pull on a pair of boots or stout walking shoes, sling a small pack on his back and be happy to be out for at least two to three hours. Many of the walks described may also appeal to family parties; to those introducing their children to the hills. For there are many facets to these walks other than the attaining of summits. There are tarns and pools for bathing, woods, waterfalls, lovely picnic spots and caves that would appeal to children. All the walks are circular, starting and finishing at the same point but returning by a different route in order to add interest. The walks described are divided into three types.

1. Valley Walks. Interesting circular valley walks are hard to find in Lakeland. The two main problems are that the nearer to valley levels the more problems with access across private or farm land, and that the very nature of Lakeland tends to force the walker uphill eventually. In all the previous booklets in this series I have managed to work out two or three. In the area covered by this booklet, however, I was unable to find a genuine and natural walk of this nature. The best I could do was a couple of half-bred, though nonetheless interesting, creations.

2. Medium Walks. These are walks that range over summits below the two-thousand feet level. They form half of the walks in this booklet for I felt they would appeal most to the kind of motorist-cum-walker family party described above. They do, however, cover similar type of ground to the fell-walks of Section Three and strictly speaking the same rules about clothing and footwear described in that section apply here. Given dry summer conditions, however, some of these walks could be done in lighter footgear, the training-type shoe, for example. It must be remembered that any Lakeland walk will have its boggy patches and that care must be taken on wet or slimy rocks at the edges of becks, rivers and waterfalls.

3. Fell Walks. These are walks that reach one or more summits over two thousand feet above sea level. They are not, however, strenuous walks of their type, either being of no great length or over relatively easy ground. Where there is any possibility of the walker getting into difficulty easier alternatives are given. Nevertheless these are fell-walks and should be treated with respect, especially in bad or winter conditions. I do not wish to labour the point but would not rest easy if I did not enumerate here a few basic rules. It is advisable to wear boots, carry a map, compass, whistle and waterproofs. In winter conditions a torch, gloves, balaclava, spare sweater, a plastic survival bag and spare food are advisable additions. Loose fitting jeans are okay in summer but warmer covering is advisable in winter. Never be afraid to turn back if the weather deteriorates and if you are forced to use your compass start using it at a point where you know where you are, then you have a fixed point to return to - don't wait until you are lost.

All the walks described are accompanied by a rough sketch-map. In clear weather, used sensibly and combined with the text, they should be more than adequate. It is advised, however, particularly for the fell-walks, to also carry the one-inch Ordnance Survey 'Tourist' Map, or the applicable sheet of the Ordnance Survey, 'The English Lakes', 1:25000 Outdoor Leisure Maps. As well as being a better aid to navigation, the Leisure Maps being particularly detailed, they also, especially the one-inch, help you to identify the various lakes and peaks seen from a particular summit or viewpoint. The mileages are approximate and 'left' or 'right' refers to an object as facing it. The parking facilities described are as at the moment of writing. Local authorities often proscribe certain areas and open up others so please don't blame the author if a particular parking situation differs from the description; it is as accurate and up to date as the author can make it.

All the walks described here are on official rights-of-way; or permissive footpaths; or on public access areas. Routes can, however, be legally changed from time to time by developments or road improvements, in which case there should be a signpost specifically indicating the alteration.

In this second edition I have revised two walks, hopefully making them more interesting than formerly. Otherwise the book remains unchanged from the original. Limited space means I have to choose between detailed route descriptions, incidental information, and detailed descriptions of views. I tend to be niggardly with the latter, feeling it's useful for walkers to attempt to orientate the view to their map.

Before I began this series of booklets my interest had always been with the high fells. If it wasn't over two thousand feet I didn't want to know. As the work has progressed, however, I have found myself becoming fascinated by hills and paths that I have to admit I had previously ignored. I only hope that the readers of this booklet discover as much pleasure from these walks as I did. Happy walking !

Tom Bowker

ULLSWATER

Walk 1

Medium Walk, 4 miles

Aira Force
and Gowbarrow Fell

Starts with one of Lakeland's most popular cascades, which really needs to be seen in spate to get the full effect. A stiffish climb follows but the views of the head of Ullswater and the fells surrounding it are superb and as the late Lakeland writer Graham Sutton wrote, "Views are like bootlaces, they are a good excuse for stopping on the way up." The broad humpy summit could give problems in thick mist without a compass and map handy.

Parking: The National Trust car-park at the foot of Aira Force. (GR 401201)

FOLLOW the path to Aira Force. After crossing the footbridge over the beck the path on the far bank divides. Take the lower left-hand path. Notice the magnificent pine trees to your left. When the walls of the gill close in the sound of cascading water will be heard ahead. Shortly the path divides again. Take the lower left-hand branch down to and across the stone bridge over the beck. Just beyond the bridge look up for a splendid view of Aira Force spanned by a higher bridge. Climb leftwards up steps and walk around to this bridge for an aerial view of the waterfall.

Continue across the bridge and turn left. When the fence on your right ends turn right and climb up steps and across grass to a footstile over a fence. Beyond this follow the path leading to the right of a lone tree, then curving up to the right between outcrops of rock. This path soon swings leftwards. To your right now is a superb view of the head of Ullswater. Directly across the lake rises Place Fell, with the lakeshore path visibly threading across its craggy base. Beyond the head of the lake rises the dome of St. Sunday Crag, and further right, above Glenridding, the dark bulk of Sheffield Pike. Above the trees below you rise the castellations of Lyulph's Tower.

As you climb, the skyline above will form two summits, a higher and rounded, to the left, a square-topped and lower, to the right. When the path divides take the fork which heads towards the rounded summit. Before reaching this top the path veers right to go behind the square summit. Beyond rises another summit, squarish and double-topped. Climb up to this. Looking back now you will see

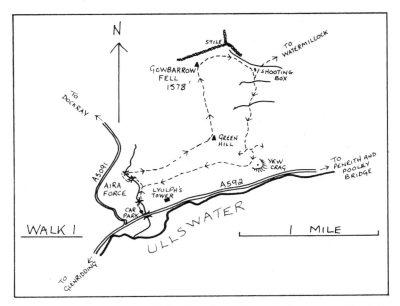

that the flat summit of Helvellyn has risen to dominate the fells above the head of the lake. Across the lake the northern fells of the High Street range are now in view beyond Place Fell. North-westerly a fluted Blencathra rises above Matterdale Common, with a flattish Skiddaw to its left and Carrock Fell to its right. Between Skiddaw and Helvellyn march the rounded Helvellyn Dods.

From this double-topped, and false, summit a path will be seen undulating up to a cairn on the far skyline. Head for this. It proves to be yet another false top, with a further cairn on the next rise. Continue to this; it is the summit of Green Hill and from it you have a view of the foot of Ullswater with the distant dome of Crossfell, monarch of the Pennines, beyond. To your left, northwards, can now be seen the rocky summit of Gowbarrow Fell crowned by an obvious trig point. The isolated rounded peak dotted with trees, seen beyond, is Great Mell Fell.

A faint path heads towards the summit, winding up and around heathery hummocks, but it has a tendency to disappear. On a clear day this is no problem but in thick mist a compass bearing from Green Hill would help. At the base of the summit mound a better path coming up from the right will be met. Follow this up to the trig point. The view is wide-ranging but nowhere near as splendid as those on the initial climb or on the return path.

To orientate yourself for the descent stand facing the National Trust sign on the trig-point. Below and to your left you will see a

7

wall which runs ahead of you, north-easterly, and down to a wall junction. Go beyond the trig-point and follow the path along the summit ridge and down in the general direction of that wall junction, which as you approach it you will see is crossed by a stile. As you approach this junction your path swings away to the right and down into a grassy ravine, with a beck to your left and a wall beyond. This path gradually improves and eventually leads down to a ruined 'shooting-box'.

Beyond the shooting-box a path is joined. Turn right, along this. This return path is delightful, traversing around the fell and gradually down and back towards Aira Force, with superb views of Ullswater below and the magnificent fells gathered at its head opening up with every turn. Shortly after leaving the shooting box it climbs across a deeply cut gill where a badly eroded section has been reinforced by fencing and wooden piles. Later it rounds a steep rocky corner before crossing another gill. A few hundred yards beyond this gill the path divides, above a grassy bay. Take the left-hand lower path which drops slightly before rising again and swinging rightwards around a corner. Ignore the steep, cairned, path dropping away to your left. Shortly a corner will be rounded with the fine cairn crowning Yew Crag slightly below to your left. This crag is used regularly by Ullswater Outward Bound Mountain School for climbing and abseiling practice. Continue round the corner to be greeted by a splendid view. Follow the path down to a junction with a lower path behind Lyulph's Tower. After passing a gate on your left the path bears rightwards towards a gate. Bear left to a stile in a fence corner. Beyond this is the Aira Force footpath.

The Helvellyn Dods

*A walk of interesting contrasts, ranging from the crowded
environs of Aira Force to the spacious grassy domes of the Helvellyn
Dods enfolding the lonely upland valley of Deepdale. The path
twisting up the flank of the Brown Hills is a delightful prelude to the
ascent of Hartside, an apparently seldom visited two thousand
footer. The Dods give easy high level walking and panoramic views.*

Parking: As for Walk 1.

FOLLOW the description given in Walk 1 as far as "Climb
leftwards up steps –". At the top of the steps turn down left then shortly
right to a gate at the edge of a wood. Follow the path through the wood
to emerge into a car park on the verge of the A5091. Cross the road to
a stile in a fence. Follow the path beyond, which slants gently left
across the fellside above Glencoyne Park. It offers a splendid view of
the head of Ullswater and its surrounding fells. Eventually a stile
leads over a wall and the path crosses the upper rim of a plantation of
splendid trees. Beyond the plantation the path twists steeply upwards
before levelling out and passing through a gap in a wall. Across
Glencoyne, Sheffield Pike blocks the view ahead.

Beyond the gap a path is joined and followed leftwards to a cairn
and path fork. Follow the right fork, cairned, across the fellside
sloping left into Glencoyne. After passing over a crossing path it
virtually disappears. Look ahead for a broken wall climbing the
fellside and head for a gap. Away to your left now, framed in the gap
between Sheffield Pike and White Stones, Catstycam's elegant cone
superimposes itself on Helvellyn's impersonation of Table Mountain.

Go through the gap in the wall. Climb alongside it for a short way
until it crosses a slight dip. Leave the wall now and climb leftwards,
west-north-westerly, up a heathery and deceptively steep fellside to
emerge onto the broad grassy south summit of Hartside. Walk north-
westerly across a slight dip to reach the cairn crowning the true
summit of Hartside, 2480 feet. The grassy cone of Great Dod, the
high point of the walk, rises challengingly ahead and barely a mile
away across the lonely swampy depths of Deepdale. Before stepping
onto this summit, however, you have to surmount the grassy domes
encircling the head of this valley. Just south of Hartside's cairn is a
stony trench, which appears to be man made but to serve what
purpose I've no idea. It does make a useful wind shelter should you
feel in need of a 'breather'.

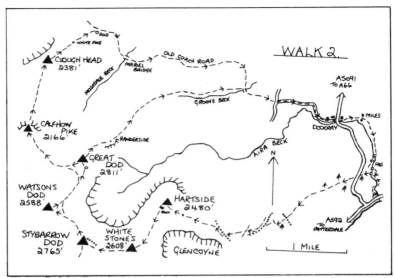

From Hartside your way is south-westerly, down onto a broad grassy saddle followed by an easy climb to the cairn crowning White Stones, 2608 feet. (On some older maps the name emblazoned on this summit is 'Greenside'). From White Stones head west down onto another broad grassy saddle followed by a pull up onto the north-eastern and highest summit of Stybarrow Dod, 2770 feet. A nearby and apparently purposeless length of wall does, however, come in useful as a wind break. Now you are upon the high grassy watershed of the Helvellyn Dods the views become panoramic. Arrayed in a great arc from Coniston Old Man to Blencathra are the cream of Lakeland's lovely lumpy high fells. From the Dods one clear September afternoon we argued whether or not it was the faint blue hills of Ireland or the Isle of Man we could see through the gap in this skyline. The unfamiliar configuration of these hills, compared to the frequently seen outline of Man, convinced me that it was Ireland. I failed to take note, however, in which gap they were framed so have no bearing to prove it.

From Stybarrow Dod a broad grassy ridge 'zigs' north-westerly to culminate in the summit of Watson's Dod, 2584 feet. It then 'zags' north-easterly to merge into the grassy summit dome of Great Dod, 2807 feet. A wind shelter just to the south of the summit cairn provides a good excuse for a 'breather'. From Great Dod there is a fine view northwards of the deeply cloven multi-ridged Threlkeld flank of Blenchathra.

Descend north-easterly down a faint but cairned path, the angle easing out onto the rocky spur of Randerside. Continue down the broad grassy ridge in roughly the same direction before swinging east and down alongside Groove Beck to join Old Coach Road. Turn right and follow this track to emerge onto a junction of tarmac roads. Now follow the road down into the hamlet of Dockray and a junction with the A5091. Cross the A5091 and go through an opening to the right of Dockray Cottage, signposted 'Aira Force/Ulcat Row'. This path passes close to the Aira Beck then between buildings at Millses before swinging right to a three-fingered signpost. Follow the 'AiraForce' indicator. The left bank of Aira Beck can be followed down to the car park. It's more interesting, however, to cross to the right bank by the footbridge near High Force, recrossing to the left bank by the bridge overlooking Aira Force and so back down to the car park.

The energetic 'peak bagger' could extend the walk by two and a half miles by descending west then north-westerly from the summit of Great Dod along the main ridge to 'bag' Calfhow Pike, 2166 feet, a brash rocky cone set amidst brawny sprawling grass domes. A more typical Dods hike just east of north also collects the summit of Clough Head, 2381 feet, where the high grassy promenade of the Helvellyn Dods comes to a precipitous end. Fine views of Skiddaw, Blencathra and the Vale of Derwentwater. Now descend north-easterly over White Pike to reach the Old Coach Road. Turn right and follow this to rejoin the description of the shorter walk, where the Coach Road crosses Groove Beck, and follow its directions to the finish.

Sheffield Pike

To the motorist driving through Patterdale from the south Sheffield Pike is the dominating fell rather than Helvellyn, which lies back from the village. From Glenridding it offers a surprisingly rocky and attractive profile. The initial climb up this relatively untrodden summit is steep, but worth the effort for the splendid views of Ullswater and the unusual but equally fine aspects of Helvellyn and Catstycam. For those interested the walk passes through the spoil-heaps and amongst the old workings of the former Greenside Lead Mine.

Parking: National Trust car-park in Glenridding (GR 386169).

WALK back out of the car park, turn left, then left again, and walk up the village street, passing the Travellers Rest pub. After leaving the houses behind the road curves right, then left, where the surface deteriorates below the first of two terraces of houses. Beyond this first terrace leave the road and follow a broad grassy path slanting towards the rear of the second terrace of houses. When just behind these houses turn right and attack the steep bracken-clad slopes above. Above and to your right a rocky bluff will be seen thrusting out of the fellside (Blaes Crag on the large O.S. map). The point where this bluff joins the main fell is your target. Climb light-coloured scree curving down the foot of the bluff, or a path to its left, above a water tank, for both head in the required direction. Just below and to the left of the neck where the bluff joins the main fell a better path, slanting across and upwards to your left, will be met. Turn left along this and follow it steeply upwards to reach a grassy saddle crowned by a wall.

Do not go through the gaps in the wall but turn left and follow a faint path climbing to the crest of the ridge on your left, where it swings right to pass through a gap in the wall. The path now zig-zags pleasantly upwards through rock and heather towards a shapely and beckoning summit. This is the summit of Heron Pike, however, not Sheffield Pike, and you may be disappointed when you reach it to find that the terrain has changed into a broad, hummocky, heathery plateau. One consolation, however, is that the hard work is now over, and another, the views. Gleaming Ullswater stretches away below you whilst away to the south-west, across the depths of the Greenside valley, shapely, aristocratic Catstycam, 'the Cat's Ladder', rises against the bulky, plebian backcloth of Helvellyn. A faint path, bearing roughly north-westerly, twists over and around the heathery hummocks, interspersed with shallow pools where dragonflies play helicopters on summer days, to meet a line of cairns on the right-hand skyline. Follow these to the summit.

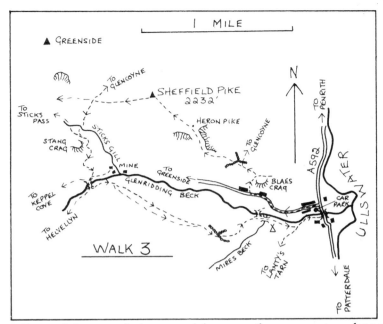

Beyond the summit the ground drops gently away westwards to a broad grassy saddle. The rounded fell beyond, its flank gashed by an old quarry, is Greenside. Behind this rises Stybarrow Dod, with the obvious gap of Sticks Pass to its left. This pass has long been a highway over the Helvellyn range and was christened after the poles that once marked it, to aid travellers and pony trains. Ore from Greenside Lead Mine was once packed over this pass to Keswick for smelting. The southern flank of Sticks Pass is guarded by Raise, at the foot of which will be seen rows of spoil-heaps, and a long culvert scarring its eastern ridge. These spoil-heaps are your next target.

Go beyond the cairn and follow a path down towards the grassy saddle. On the saddle your path curves right and down into a grassy cleft to a junction with a crossing path. Turn left along this path, climbing out of the cleft, and follow it south-westerly and down to the edge of Sticks Gill, where it runs below the spoil-heaps. Cross the gill by stepping-stones, or an old footbridge up-beck, and walk up the far bank to meet a better path crossing below the spoil-heaps. Turn left and follow this. The path bears right and then zig-zags down the edges of the steep, massive spoil-heaps overlooking the old mine buildings, now an outdoor pursuits centre. After passing under Stang Crag and through a belt of dwarf juniper head down to the footbridge over the Glenridding Beck, above and to the right of the buildings. Cross this and turn left along a path traversing the

13

flank of Birkhouse Moor, and parallel to the beck and road below. Eventually this path is blocked-off, due to erosion, and a signpost directs you down to a stile/gate in a wall corner. Beyond this follow the path down to a rough farm road and continue down this to see a small stone bridge on your right signposted 'Car-Park' on its left wall. Cross this and follow a path between the beck and the camp-site to a T-junction. Turn left and follow the lane back to Glenridding.

Walk 4   **Fell Walk, 8-9 miles**

The Helvellyn Edges

Striding Edge is undoubtedly the most popular way up Helvellyn from the east. It is the lure that attracts walkers of all ages and all standards to this side of the moutain. It would be impossible to leave it out of any walking guidebook to the Ullswater area. A traverse of Striding Edge takes a step beyond simple fellwalking. Given dry, calm conditions, however, the reader of this booklet who has done the Rough Crag – Long Stile ridge and the St. Sunday Crag – Cofa Pike ridge should have no problem. The round of Striding Edge and Swirrel Edge gives one of the most exciting day's fellwalking that Lakeland can offer.

Parking: As for walk 3.

GO back to the main road, turn right over the bridge, and right again up the lane past the climbing shop. Continue until the path forks. Take the right-hand fork, signposted 'Greenside', to go between the beck and the campsite to reach and cross a stone bridge. Beyond this turn left up a rough track alongside a wall to a gate/stile signposted 'Helvellyn via Mires Beck'. Cross this and climb left to a similar sign on a wall directing you right up to a gate/stile in a wall corner. Beyond this turn left across a footbridge over a beck. Now climb the path up the right bank of Mires Beck, shortly crossing over to the left bank. A long steepish climb follows, the path eventually climbing alongside a wall, before the grassy summit of Birkhouse Moor, 2353 feet, is attained. The view back of the constant changes of light on the shining reaches of Ullswater is a good excuse for 'breathers'. Some 'peak-baggers' lists credit Birkhouse Moor with three summits but I feel that's a trifle generous. My list makes the highest point just to the right of the wall corner where the wall veers south-westerly towards Striding Edge. The 2½" map argues for the next bump that way – take your pick!

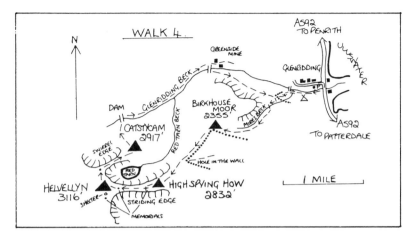

Hopefully, displayed before you now are the famous 'edges', enfolding the high corrie cupping Red Tarn and airily linking Helvellyn's 'table mountain' with conical Catstycam. Perhaps I should liken Helvellyn more to a giant aircraft carrier. In 1926 two daring young men landed their flying machine upon its summit then, more daringly, took off from it. A memorial to this feat stands just south of the summit shelter.

Continue, a little swampily, alongside the wall until it turns away at the Hole-in-the-Wall and you start the climb towards Striding Edge. Leave the worn path and climb the obvious summit overlooking the start of the 'edge' proper. This is High Spying How, 2832 feet, and listed as a separate peak.

Once on Striding Edge the way is obvious. Don't be deterred by the metal cross just below and to the left after the first narrow section, a memorial to an unfortunate follower of foxhounds, the danger is more apparent than real. Unless you find it too scary, or ice and snow conditions forcibly prevent it, attempt to keep to the crest all the way. This gives the excitement, fun and satisfaction that is the point of an ascent by this route. The most difficult section is the climb down into the gap at the end of the Edge, but even here the holds are large and firm. Beyond this gap there is another hump of rock to scramble over and then the route degenerates into a steep, shaly pant up onto the fell rim, emerging near a memorial to a doggy who maintained a long and loyal vigil over the corpse of his master, earning poetic praise from Wordsworth and Sir Walter Scott. There is a school of thought, admittedly largely composed of cat lovers, who believe faithful Fido fortified himself with a bit of Master!

Walk right along the rim of the fell shortly to reach the invariably crowded wind shelter just below the summit. Climb up onto the summit rocks of Helvellyn, 3116 feet. The view from Helvellyn is panoramic and I have not the space to describe it. It is a good place, on a clear windless day, to take your map and orientate yourself to the splendours of Lakeland spread at your feet.

Walk north-westerly along the rim, passing the slightly lower trig-point, to a cairn on the rim, where it veers west-south-westerly, marking the start of the descent onto Swirrel Edge. After heavy snowfalls, large cornices build up along this rim. In 'white-out' conditions they can, and have been, death traps for the unwary. Swirrel Edge is much easier and shorter than its big brother across Red Tarn, only a couple of rocky steps requiring care. At its lowest point a path forks right, down towards Red Tarn. Ignore this and climb along the ridge, broad and easy now, onto the narrow summit of Catstycam, 2917 feet, a graceful, relatively unfrequented peak, a splendid viewpoint, and worth every gasp of extra effort.

Turn left and descend a steepish stony path down the fell's north west ridge to a 'busted' dam spanning the Glenridding Beck. In the 1920's water was stored in Keppel Cove, to your left, to power the Greenside Lead Mine smelters. The dam burst, loosing millions of gallons of water which, clawing up boulders and trees en route, poured into Glenridding village causing extensive damage but fortunately no loss of life. Cross the crest of the dam. If it's at all gusty you will probably regard this crossing as more scary than anything on the famous 'edges'. I know I have.

Follow the track on the far side down to the buildings of the old Greenside Lead Mine, now an outdoor pursuits centre. The mine was in production from 1780 to 1962, producing over one quarter of a million tones of lead concentrate. Just above the buildings cross back over the Glenridding Beck by a footbridge and turn left along a pleasant path traversing below the steep craggy Blea Cove flank of Birkhouse Moor to rejoin your outward route at a gate/stile.

Warning: When plastered with snow and ice this walk is a different proposition. It should not be attempted without the proper equipment, ice axe, crampons, and possibly a rope, and the ability to use them.

Place Fell and the
Ullswater shore-path

A fairly long but entertaining walk which is nowhere strenuous, all the hard work being done in the first three miles. The view from Place Fell is superb and on the flanks of this isolated fell there is always the chance of spotting red deer. The shore path is delightful, possibly the best of its kind in Lakeland, offering more fine, and constantly changing, views and the opportunity of a swim or a lakeside picnic.

Parking: The car park behind the AA Box, near Cow Bridge, over the Goldrill Beck, on the A592 about a mile and a half south of Patterdale. (GR 403134).

GO back to the road, turn right and follow it to where a minor road, signposted 'Hartsop', branches left. Turn down this and after passing a white house turn left into a walled lane. Follow this lane, for about half a mile, to a gate. Beyond the gate a path continues, crossing a footbridge over the Angle Tarn Beck. Continue to where the path divides. Take the path climbing up to your right. The left-hand fork is your eventual return route. The path eventually crosses a beck, Stonebarrow Gill, channelled between stones, to join with a path coming up from Patterdale. Turn right and climb up to reach Boardale Hause, a flattish area, above and to the left of a spoil heap, which is decorated with a variety of cairns.

Walk into the far left-hand corner of this area, passing a metal manhole cover. Beyond this the path swings left to pass a small sheepfold and head towards the steep summit slopes of Place Fell. Soon the path veers left and climbs steeply up the edge of the skyline to reach a gully leading to the cairn on Round How. The summit can now be seen a short distance beyond and is easily reached by following a worn path running along the edge of the fell. The all-round views from the cairn are superb. This is an ideal spot for taking out your map and orientating yourself with Lakeland's eastern fells. The high point, for me, is the detailed panorama of the rugged ice-honed eastern flanks of Fairfield and Helvellyn. North-westerly, Blencathra displays its fluted Threlkeld flank, with a retiring flat-topped Skiddaw to its left. Further north, through the gap between isolated Great Mell Fell and Carrock Fell, lie the Solway Firth and Scotland.

To descend, continue in the same direction beyond the summit following a path to a pointed and cairned feature christened The Knight. Beyond this the path veers north-easterly, down a rocky groove, before dropping more steeply down to the sheepfold on the grassy saddle of Low Moss. Pass to the right of the sheepfold and when the path forks turn left and follow the path down the right bank of Low Moss Gill. The path improves as you descend and eventually passes a derelict quarry building. Below this building the path splits. Keep to the left-hand fork. Across to your left Scalehow Beck tumbles out of a hanging valley to merge with Low Moss Gill. Your path heads down towards the fine cascades below this junction. Ahead the view down the lower reaches of Ullswater widens impressively with every turn of the path. The path touches the edges of the beck then swings away to the right where it passes between some large boulders. Hereabouts it splits, with a fork heading down steep grass to meet a lower path. Go down this fork. Turn left along the lower path to cross Scalehow Beck by a footbridge. Beyond the bridge the path climbs up towards a gate then swings left just before reaching it to climb steeply up alongside a wall. Follow the path around the wall corner and when it divides take the upper fork. The prominent fell across the lake is Gowbarrow Fell; along the lakeshore at its foot Wordsworth saw his famed daffodils. The castle-like structure is Lyulph's Tower.

As the path picks its delightful way across the steep, rocky, lake-lapped base of Place Fell the view ahead constantly varies. At first the eye looks deep into Glencoynedale, guarded by Greenside and the dark rocky bulk of Sheffield Pike. As you go, Birkhouse Moor, Catstycam and the eastern ridges of Nethermost Pike and Dollywaggon Pike slowly march into view. Roughly a mile and a half after rounding the wall corner Silver Bay and its pebbly beach is reached. Here the path divides near a large cairn. Take the left-hand path, up a rocky ravine, to reach a grassy saddle and fine viewpoint. Distantly ahead is the gap of Kirkstone Pass, dividing John Bell's Banner, on the left, from Red Screes. Below, in the foreground, is Patterdale village. Further right, across the head of Ullswater, you look into Grisedale, with distant Seat Sandal at its head. To its left St. Sunday Crag bulks large, whilst to its right are arrayed the fine eastern coves and ridges of Dollywaggon Pike, Nethermost Pike and Striding Edge. Your way ahead lies along the path traversing the fellside. It is well-constructed and as you go you will realise why, passing below, above and through derelict slate quarries.

When this path forks continue with the left-hand path slanting across the fellside. It passes an iron seat, dips down, near an old quarry, then divides, with a branch curving down to the right. Ignore this right-hand fork and continue leftwards, crossing the site of another old quarry before dropping down to a footbridge over a beck. Cross the footbridge and go through a gate into a lane. Turn left down the lane, between houses. When the lane bears right look for a lane on your left. On the left of this lane, on the wall of Rooking Gill Barn, there should be a sign 'Hartsop. Unfit for Cars'.

Follow this lane, between houses and a fence. Pass through a gateway, then between farm buildings, and before reaching a white house look for a slate sign on your left 'Footpath to Hartsop', near a stile with an iron bar in it. Cross the stile, followed by a footbridge over a beck. The path now follows a fence and swings around to the right to reach a stile, on your left. Cross this stile and go to the left of a barn, then between a wall and a fence, then over a stile, to reach a farm track. Opposite the stile you will see a slate sign 'Hartsop'. Follow this track to meet a stile and gate leading into the farmyard of Beckstones. Go through the farmyard and pass through a gateway to reach a fork in the path. Take the left-hand fork shortly to join your outward route.

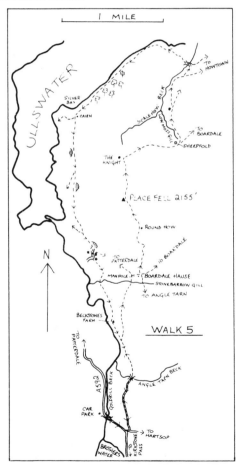

Hallin Fell

An easy walk combining a superb viewpoint with a delightful lakeshore stroll. Can be done independently or combined with Walk Seven, Pikewassa and Martindale, to make a longer and even more varied expedition.

Parking: From Pooley Bridge take the road signposted 'Howtown', along the south-eastern shore of Ullswater. Park in the old quarry on the right of the road just beyond the crest of the fierce Howtown zig-zags, and opposite St. Peter's church. (GR 435193).

FOLLOW the worn grassy path starting from the left-hand end of the quarry. A short distance above the start you pass, on your left, a wall corner, where a drystone wall veers away across the flank of the fell. Store this detail in your memory.

Hallin Fell is crowned by a beautifully contructed cairn. The all-round view is superb, although somewhat restricted to the south and east by the neighbouring fells. Below you Ullswater stretches out its shining levels to either hand. Stand facing the lake and the neighbouring fell to your left is Place Fell. To the right of this, but distantly, can be seen a flat-topped Helvellyn framed between Striding Edge, on the left, and the delectably sculpted Catstycam. Below and to the right of Catstycam the dark bulk of Sheffield Pike overlooks Glenridding. The rounded Helvellyn Dods march away from Sheffield Pike towards distant Skiddaw. East of Skiddaw rises gracefully fluted Blencathra followed by its more mundane neighbours Bannerdale Crags and Bowscale Fell. In the foreground Gowbarrow Fell looms over the lake, with the tree-dotted dome of Great Mell Fell to its right. Away to your right the hamlet of Pooley Bridge nestles at the foot of Ullswater with the distant Pennines rising beyond. Blocking the eastern view is neighbouring, beacon-topped, Bonscale Pike, a northern 'tail-ender' of the long High Street range. This range marches away southwards in a succession of bulky fells the farthest of which, Rampsgill Head, commanding the head of Martindale, hides High Street. In the foreground perky Pikewassa splits the lower reaches of Martindale from narrow Fusedale, tucked in the shadow of Loadpot Hill. Lower Martindale is dominated by The Nab, above and beyond which Rest Dod, an insignificant fell from most viewpoints, shows a fine profile. The craggy ridge of Beda Fell divides Martindale from Boardale. This ridge is topped by the startlingly spiky summit, seen from this viewpoint, of the highest Angle Tarn Pike. Bulky Place Fell forms Boardale's western wall and we have come the full scenic circle.

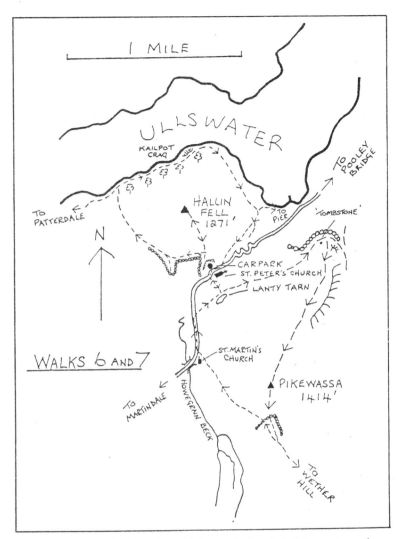

After digesting this splendid feast of visual delights return down to the previously mentioned wall corner. Turn right here and make your way along faint paths through the bracken, alongside the wall. After about four hundred yards the wall turns downhill, whilst ahead a further wall comes up to take its place. In the gap between these walls a better path, slanting up from the left, will be met. Follow this path, to go alongside a wall and eventually down into trees and a junction with a lakeshore path just to the right of a gate. Turn right and follow the shore path, always keeping to the left when any apparent diversion appears. Beyond an obvious rocky headland, Kailpot Crag, the path emerges from the trees and begins to slant rightwards and uphill, eventually with a wall on its left. Ignore a gate in this wall, with an obvious footpath beyond, and continue following the wall. Shortly the path divides. Take the broad grassy right-hand path which climbs steadily uphill, aloof to the squealing tyres and the grinding gears on the nearby zig-zags, to return you to your car.

An interesting climax to the day is to stroll across the road and visit the beautifully maintained little upland church of St. Peter's of Martindale.

Walk 7   **Medium Walk, 3 miles**

Pikewassa and Martindale

Less frequented than neighbouring Hallin Fell, Walk 6, with which it could be combined. Demands a little more 'puff' but worth the effort for the view from its pleasant summit ridge and spiky top. For those interested in such things the old church of St. Martin, with its once-pagan font and eight hundred years old yew tree, only adds more pleasure to an enjoyable short walk.

Parking: As for Walk Six.

WALK to the right of the church, and alongside a wall, to reach tiny Lanty Tarn. Turn left here and follow a good grassy path which slants gently down across the fellside. Eventually a wall climbs up from the left to run alongside the path. Now keep your eyes open for a small metal manhole cover in the path with a tombstone-like stone marker on the right of the path, just before a rocky outcrop on your right.

Climb the bank above the 'tombstone' onto a sloping grassy shelf. Look for a narrow path climbing slightly right. Follow this path which climbs steeply to the right of the rocks above. Eventually the angle eases, the odd cairn appears, and the path improves to follow the crest of a pleasant, rock-encrusted ridge. Pause for a breather and a fine view back down the lower reaches of Ullswater.

Continue your climb, with the angle easing, the ridge broadening and the view expanding with every upward step. To your right, across the deep furrows of Martindale and Boardale, looms Place Fell. A keen eye might spot the topmost spire of Catstycam peeking over its rim. Left of Place Fell, St. Sunday Crag dramatically fills the gap in the skyline left by Boardale Hause. Tucked in behind St. Sunday Crag is higher Fairfield, with Cofa Pike perched like a parrot on its shoulder. Ahead, beyond the fell crest, The Nab spires out of the depths of Martindale, with Rest Dod looming above and beyond. Far Rampsgill Head, the northern bastion of High Street and 'King of the Martindale Fells', blocks the head of the valley. To your left, across the depths of the lonely valley of Fusedale, rise the brawny gill-furrowed flanks of Loadpot Hill and Wether Hill.

Continue beyond the last cairn to reach the spiky rocks that form the summit of Pikewassa. Follow the path beyond the summit and down to pass through a gap in a wall. Then turn right and descend steeply alongside the wall to shortly reach a lower, well-used, path.

Pause here and look left down into Martindale where a red-roofed building will be spotted rising above the trees. This is The Bungalow, formerly a shooting-lodge of the Earls of Lonsdale, where The Kaiser, Wilhelm II, stayed as a guest prior to the First World War. Ironically, during the Second World War, it sheltered the somewhat spartan Officers' Mess of a battle camp established in the valley. The sparse trees clinging to the fellside below your feet are reputedly one of the remaining areas of relict or native woodland left in Lakeland.

Now turn right and follow the path pleasantly down to the rear of the old church of St. Martin. A visit to this plain, sturdy upland chapel, with its quiet atmosphere of devotion and history, is a highlight of this walk.

Leaving the church, follow the road towards Howtown. About four hundred yards on look for a gate, signposted 'Footpath to Howtown' on the wall to its right. Go through the gate and follow the path beyond to the dwelling at 'Cotehow'. Pass to the front of the house, across its drive, and climb a grassy path around to a gate and shortly beyond to reach Lanty Tarn. The church of St. Peter, near the car park, is also worth a visit, though it lacks the atmosphere of times past.

St. Sunday Crag,
Cofa Pike and Fairfield

A splendid high-level walk giving superb and constantly changing views, and a flavour of mountaineering in the crossing of Cofa Pike. Undoubtedly the finest of the ridges radiating from Fairfield. In hard winter conditions, however, this route should not be attempted without an ice-axe, and the ability to use it. A 'white-out', snow combined with mist, turns the Fairfield summit plateau into a hazardous place. In such conditions careful attention must be paid to navigation.

Parking: There is limited parking space at the foot of the lane leading into Grisedale, near the playing field. (GR 391162). Otherwise it's park where you can without causing offence, or traffic-jams, or drive on to the Glenridding car-park.

WALK up the winding lane for about half a mile. After passing a white house, on your right, a gate will be seen on your left signposted 'Public Footpath'. Go through this and shortly beyond bear right, either through a metal gate or over a stile, and follow the path climbing steeply up the fellside. This passes through trees before emerging onto the open fell once more. Behind, there is a fine view down onto the head of Ullswater. Beyond the far ridge of Grisedale, its flank scarred by the worn 'trod' slanting up towards Striding Edge, rise high shapely Catstycam and bluff lowly Sheffield Pike.

Continue to a stile over a wall. Beyond this the path flanks across a steep fellside for about three hundred yards before dividing, near a cairn. The lower, right-hand path circumvents the outlying summit of Birks. Unless time is short I see no merit in this for Birks is the natural beginning to this fine ridge. Climb steeply up to the left, the path bearing further left as the angle eases, before curving back rightwards towards the small cairn that crowns the broad grassy summit. The dominating feature of the view is the challenging profile of St. Sunday Crag, your next objective. Dove Crag and Hart Crag, Fairfield outliers, peer around its left-hand profile and Helvellyn has now expanded in more detail to its right.

Head easily down to the saddle below St. Sunday Crag and a junction with the flanking path previously mentioned. The summit is reached by climbing directly up the ridge ahead or by a path, which appears to have lost favour over the years, slanting leftwards across the face of the fell. The cairn stands near the southern rim of

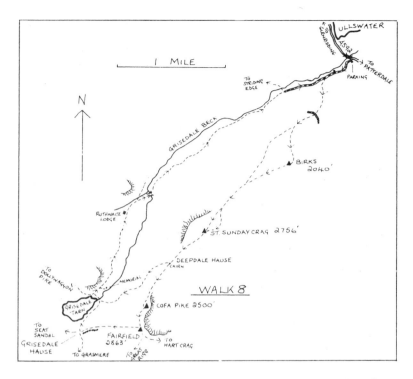

the stony summit dome. Helvellyn, Striding Edge and the splendid coves and ridges of Dollywaggon and Nethermost Pikes are seen to advantage from here. Dominating the scene, however, is the rugged, massive north-east face of Fairfield, particularly if draped in snow. Cofa Pike, your next target, virtually disappears into the stark backcloth of its giant neighbour.

Go south-westerly along a ridge which steepens and narrows as it drops on to Deepdale Hause. It has been my frequent experience to meet a strong wind on this section of the ridge. Presumably the prevailing westerlies, frustrated by the mountain wall of Helvellyn and Fairfield, scream into the gap filled by Grisedale Tarn, ahead and below, and are funnelled directly at Deepdale Hause. On the hause a cairn marks the beginning of a path which slants down to reach Grisedale Tarn near its exit beck. This is a useful escape route if required.

Steep rocky climbing follows to reach the narrow and enjoyable summit ridge of Cofa Pike. Beyond, a short dip is followed by a stiffish scree slope to reach the broad summit plateau of Fairfield. The view is extensive. Highlights are the gleaming waters of

Windermere, Esthwaite and Coniston to the south; beyond glints Morecambe Bay. Westerly the thrusting dome of Gable dominates a superb mountain skyline ranging from Coniston Old Man to Grisedale Pike. Helvellyn and its splendid outliers sprawl across the northern sky. From the north-eastern rim there is an interesting bird's-eye view into rugged Sleet Cove, dominated by Hutaple Crag. This rim is where the danger lies in a 'white-out', for large cornices build up here.

Two stone 'shelters' crown Fairfield, one balanced on the north-eastern rim, the other further west and more central. North of this second shelter a cairn stands on a rocky plinth. From this latter cairn a line of cairns heads west, across the plateau. Follow these. They lead to a steep and eroded path which eventually runs down alongside an old wall and into the narrow saddle of Grisedale Hause. The fell rising steeply beyond is Seat Sandal.

Turn right here and follow the path past the dark waters of Grisedale Tarn. Legend has it that the huge cairn on Dunmail Raise marks the site of the battle where Dunmail, the last native king of Cumberland, was defeated by the Anglo-Saxons. Survivors from the slaughter are reputed to have fled up to Grisedale Tarn where they flung Dunmail's crown into the water. Their ghosts are purported to repeat this act. Fact or fiction, the truth lies somewhere between, for history tells us that King Dunmail died in Rome, with his boots on.

Cross Grisedale Beck, where it issues from the tarn, by stepping stones. Notice the escape route from Deepdale Hause coming down to your right. Beyond the beck the path swings right and down, under the steep buttresses of Tarn and Falcon Crags. Shortly after beginning the descent from the tarn look across to your right to spot a T-shaped metal memorial crowning an outcrop of rock. This is known as The Brothers' Parting. Here Wordsworth is said to have bid farewell to his younger and sailor brother John who was subsequently drowned in a shipwreck.

The path continues down to pass Ruthwaite Lodge, now the weekend home of the Sheffield University Mountaineering Club. This now well-maintained structure was a chilly shell, deep in sheep droppings, when I first sought shelter in it on a wild winter's day in 1951. Behind the hut lovely cascades spill out of the lonely recesses of Ruthwaite Cove. Below the hut the path divides. Take the right fork which leads down to a footbridge over the Grisedale Beck. The path now leads you pleasantly back down the valley and eventually to your car. Glance back occasionally at the splendid mix of sharp ridges and rugged hanging valleys.

BROTHERSWATER

Walk 9   **Fell Walk, 7 miles**

Dovedale, Dove Crag, and Caiston Glen

An enjoyable and not particularly strenuous walk passing through some rugged mountain scenery. Walls and fences are a useful aid to navigation in the upper reaches.

Parking: As for Walk Five.

WALK to the rear of the car-park, crossing the bridge over the Goldrill Beck, and turn left through the gate on to the track leading along the wooded western shore of Brotherswater. This track eventually passes Hartsop Hall, the site of a dwelling place since the thirteenth century, to join with the path from the campsite behind the Brotherswater Hotel. Continue, passing to the right of sheep pens and farm buildings and a gate signposted 'Footpath to Kirkstone Pass and Scandale Pass'. This gate marks where your return route will emerge. Just beyond these buildings the track forks. Take the right-hand path signposted 'Dove Crag'. This climbs up into the trees, passing below the ruins of an old lead mine. After about half a mile the woods end at a wall. Beyond it the valley ahead can be seen to narrow and swing to the left, with the path clinging to its right wall. Immediately above, to your right, are the clean rocks of Dovedale Slabs or Gill Crag. A handful of amiable rock-climbs are recorded on them. At the end of the valley can be seen aptly named Black Crag, which acts as a drainage channel for the upper fell and is invariably discoloured with seeping water.

The scene which greets the eye, as you follow the path as it twists and climbs to the left at the end of the valley, is as wild and magnificent as any in Lakeland. Towering ahead, above a sweep of scree and a tumble of massive weathered boulders, is the stark face of Dove Crag. It has not the massiveness of Scafell Crag, Pavey Ark or Dow, but its line is relentless and many of Britain's finest climbers have been drawn by its immutable challenge. Shortly after crossing a beck the path bears right and several hundred feet of steep climbing up a grassy groove bounded by thrusting ribs of rock follows. This steep section ends with a wet rocky corner, which can be avoided. Beyond this grassy slopes fall back and from this point an interesting diversion can be made by those with a steady head for heights. Turn left and cross grass and scree to where an obvious rocky rake leads around onto the face of Dove Crag. This leads up to a surprisingly large cave. A dozen or so people could bivouac quite comfortably here, and often do, so please don't leave any litter. There is a theory bandied about that it is not a natural cave but a 'priest hole', hacked or blasted out by dalesmen loyal to the Old Faith. I have been unable to find any proof of this but one can climb to within feet of the cave mouth without becoming aware of its existence. It cannot be seen from the valley and one has to climb high on the Hartsop-above-How ridge before its dark mouth is spotted. From the cave entrance, however, there is a bird's-eye view of Dovedale. On a clear day nothing that moved in Dovedale could fail to be observed by a watcher here. It is an exciting thought for the romantics among us.

Return to the path, if you've elected to leave it, and follow it around to the left of a boggy basin which frequently holds a shallow tarn. Soon steeper climbing and cairns lead to the wall crowning the saddle between Dove Crag and Hart Crag. Turn left and follow the wall for around a third of a mile to where the summit cairn of Dove Crag's undistinguished top will be seen on your left. The view is extensive save to the north-west where it is blocked by Fairfield.

For the descent continue along the wall until a fence is met bearing away to the left. Follow this, keeping to its right, and making sure you are not ambushed by the occasional tentacles of rusting wire it treacherously snakes out. After a steepish section, and beyond where another fence joins from the left, your fence turns south-east. Roughly a third of a mile on the fence veers more southerly. The peak rising immediately to your left is Little Hart Crag, an isolated, surprisingly rocky and seldom visited two-thousand footer. Follow the fence down, passing to the left of an un-named tarn, to a junction with a wall. Turn left alongside the wall, then shortly right, to follow it down to reach the stile crowning the crest of Scandale Pass.

Turn left here and follow the path down into Caiston Glen, where the Caiston Beck spills down towards Brotherswater in a delightful sequence of frothy cascades and clear pools. A mile and a half below the pass, at the foot of Little Hart Crag's north-east ridge, the path passes to the right of an old barn signposted 'To campsite and Patterdale'. The hoary monoliths scattered around the meadow beyond are reputedly the relics of an ancient stone circle. A footbridge leads across the Harstop Beck and after passing through a sequence of gates to the right of farm buildings your outward route is joined.

For those still feeling energetic when Scandale Pass is reached the walk could be extended to 'bag' Red Screes. To do this walk past the stile and follow the wall up the fellside to a junction with a crossing wall. Go through a gap in this and head, just north of east,

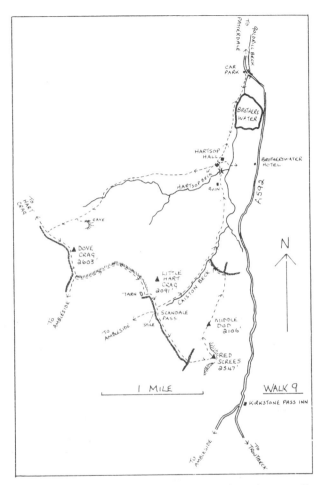

over easy grass to reach the trig point perched on the very lip of the precipitous north-east flank, beyond a small shallow tarn. The aerial northern view, towards Brotherswater, and south, down the island-studded gleam of Windermere, make the extra effort worthwhile. To descend, head northwards around the rim of the fell. A faint path leads down to a grassy saddle and up to the summit of Middle Dod. Beyond this continue down the steep ridge until a crossing wall is met. Turn left and follow this steeply down into Caiston Glen to cross the beck and join the path already described. It must be said that from Middle Dod down to Caiston Glen is steep knee-jellying work with little definite in the way of a path.

29

John Bell's Banner,
Thresthwaite Cove and Hartsop

John Bell's Banner looks like a 'pudden' of a fell from most angles but it is one for the connoisseur, continually revealing interesting facets for those who trouble to look. An enjoyable and varied short walk with all the hard work over in the first mile.

Parking: In the lay-by just north of the bridge over the Caudale Beck, about quarter of a mile south of the Brotherswater Hotel, on the A592. (GR 403115).

GO through the metal gate on the south side of the bridge and follow the path above and parallel to the beck. After a while it spirals right onto a steep, well-defined grassy ridge. This zig-zagging hollowed path is the remains of an old 'sledgate' and eventually it slants away along the left flank of the ridge to reach ruined quarry buildings overlooking the lonely hanging valley of Caudale. Men used to steer sleds, or trailbarrows, loaded with a quarter of a ton of slate down this path, running before them like a horse, then hauling the empty sled back uphill and repeating the performance. One Honister quarryman, Joseph Clarke of Stonethwaite, is recorded as having shifted five tons of slate and covered seventeen miles in seventeen successive journeys.

If you slant left and explore the ruins be careful as there is at least one crudely covered and evil-looking hole. The high mountain sanctuary of Caudale is a favourite feeding place for red deer. Climb back up the crest of the ridge to regain the path. Behind and below you lies Brotherswater, with a glimpse of Ullswater beyond. Across the A592 you look into the depths of Dovedale, dominated by the pale steep walls of Dove Crag, with the eastern skyline of Fairfield and St. Sunday Crag rising beyond.

Continue up the ridge which gradually levels out into the summit plateau where a large cairn, marked 2,474 feet on both large and small O.S. maps, is reached. Easterly, beyond a small tarn, stone walls crowd the skyline. Head south-east to meet the wall and path climbing up from Kirkstone Pass. Turn left and follow this to reach the junction of walls that crowns the broad sumit of this fell. Go through a gap in the crossing wall to reach the cairn. To the north-west there is a distant but comprehensive view of the rugged eastern flanks of Fairfield and Helvellyn. To the east, across Threshthwaite Mouth, the graceful summit cairn of Thornthwaite Crag beckons, with the dome of High Street to its left. Froswick and Ill Bell look

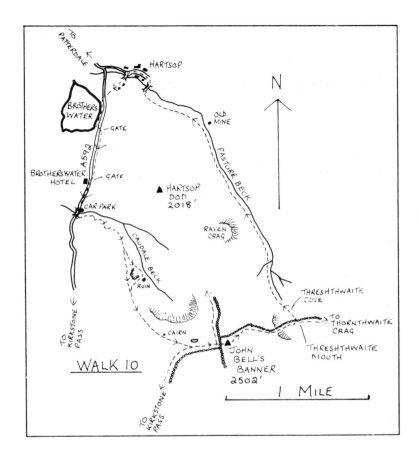

their shapely best to the south-east and below them the green hollow of Troutbeck leads the eye down to gleaming Windermere.

This sprawling fell has two other names, Caudale Moor and Stony Cove Pike, but I prefer the bold ringing sound of John Bell's Banner. About 350 years ago the curate of Ambleside was one John Bell and his parish boundary ran across the summit of this fell. The local name for boundary being 'banner' this mountain signified, in the eyes of his flock, the limit of both his spiritual and temporal ministrations.

For the descent head north-east to meet a wall. Path and wall now accompany each other down to the grassy saddle of

31

Threshthwaite Mouth. The last few hundred feet are steep and rocky. Exercise caution or discretion here in adverse conditions. At Threshthwaite Mouth turn left through the first gap in the wall to pass a small cairn and meet a path leading down into the drumlin-dimpled hollow of Threshthwaite Cove. Ullswater may be glimpsed beyond the valley mouth. The path drops out of Threshthwaite Cove and threads through the boulderfield scattered below the pronounced overhangs of Raven Crag, then levels out to follow the left bank of Pasture Beck. Eventually a stile is crossed and as the now broader track climbs away from the beck look over the wall to your right to see, on the further bank, the ruins of an old lead mine. The track continues bearing left, alongside a wall, before swinging right and down to cross a packhorse bridge over the Pasture Beck. Beyond, it goes up onto a car-park and then into the picturesque hamlet of Hartsop.

With its spinning-galleries, old corn-drying kiln, allied to the neighbouring ruins of a lead mine and the old quarry workings in Caudale, Hartsop retains aspects of a time when many of Lakeland's loveliest corners were self-sufficient units of rural industry. As you follow the road through the hamlet look for a gap between buildings on your left leading down to a footbridge back over the Pasture Beck. Cross this and follow the delightful lane beyond which eventually brings you out onto the A592. Cross the road and go through a kissing-gate signposted 'National Trust, Brotherswater'. Beyond this bear left and follow a path along the wooded eastern shore of the lake which eventually climbs back up onto the road. Turn right along the road for a short distance keeping your eyes open for a kissing-gate signposted 'National Trust' opposite. Go through this and turn right to follow a path running above and parallel to the road.

When opposite the Brotherswater Hotel gates lead back onto the road. You could take advantage of these to down a refreshing pint before walking the few hundred yards back up the road to your car.

Angle Tarn Pikes, Angle Tarn and Hayes Water

An amiable walk with all the hard work in the first mile or so. Interesting views. Angle Tarn is a delightful spot for a picnic or swim. From the steep zig-zags of the A592, below Kirkstone Pass, the rugged profiles of Angle Tarn Pikes give excellent imitations of mini-volcanoes.

Parking: As for Walks Five and Nine.

FOLLOW the directions for Walk Five, Place Fell and the Ullswater shore-path, as far as 'Boardale Hause, a flattish area, above and to the left of a spoil heap, which is decorated with a variety of cairns'. Turn right here and follow the well-worn path, re-crossing Stonebarrow Gill, above and to the left of a sheepfold. This path twists and climbs between grassy hillocks before the ground on the right falls steeply away to give a splendid view down on to Brotherswater, with the spirals of the Kirkstone Pass road, dominated by Red Screes, rising beyond. Shortly afterwards the path forks, near a sign 'Angle Tarn'. Both paths in fact lead to the tarn.

If you wish to 'bag' Angle Tarn Pikes, however, follow the sign and turn left. This path climbs and swings to the right, passing below the summits and continuing on to the tarn. At a convenient point turn left and climb steeply up to reach the narrow northern, and highest, top. The view is restricted by the surrounding higher fells but is nevertheless full of variety. There is splendid depth in the south-west arc, looking down onto Brotherswater and into the valleys of Dovedale and Deepdale.

Walk north-easterly along the summit ridge to drop down and turn right into the boggy hollow dividing the Pikes. Climb up to the southern top for a fine view of Angle Tarn. Head down towards the tarn and a junction once more with the more well-trodden path. A grassy promontory in the north-east corner provides a splendid picnic site or bathing platform. From here there is an interesting view of the eastern flank of flat-topped Fairfield framed between the rocky hillocks encircling the tarn, with rounded Cofa Pike tucked up close under its summit to the right and Hart Crag to its left.

To continue with the walk follow the path slanting upwards above the eastern shore of the tarn. As you climb the view across the tarn expands to fill the skyline with the rugged eastern aspect of the

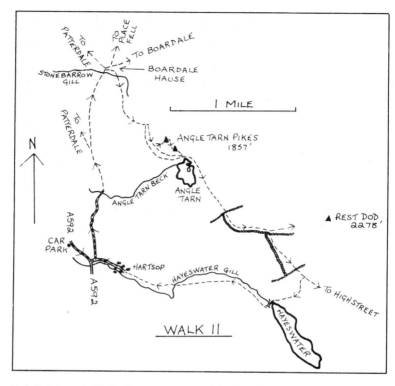

WALK II

Fairfield and Helvellyn ranges, with the fine cone of Catstycam predominant. When the path begins to level off the fells glimpsed ahead are broad-backed John Bell's Banner, criss-crossed by walls, and the more aggresively thrusting Grey Crag. Below and to the left of the latter peak Hayes Water will be glimpsed, tucked into its shadowy combe under High Street. Soon after a crossing wall is seen the path swings left to pass through a gate in a wall corner.

The path, with a wall now to its right, undulates along a broad rocky ridge. Below and to the right lies Hayes Water whilst to the left are deep, occasional glimpses into Bannerdale, with perhaps a peep of Ullswater beyond. Ahead rises the grassy summit of Rest Dod, with the shadow streaked, ramshackle pinnacles of Rampsgill Head above and to the right. The wall to the right gives way to a fence as the foot of Rest Dod is approached. Then the path and fence swing abruptly right to flank this little visited, in my experience, two-thousand footer. The energetic may 'bag' it by heading steeply uphill, alongside a wall, from the point where the path veers abruptly right, returning the same way.

The less energetic should continue with the walk as planned. After the abrupt turn the path continues to climb gradually, slanting leftwards across the flank of the fell. The fence on your right has now given way to a wall and the path begins to veer away from this to go through a gap in a crossing wall. After passing through this gap you will cross a boggy area. Beyond this leave the path, which heads up towards High Street, and turn down the fellside to your right. Slant leftwards towards the dam at the foot of Hayes Water and shortly you will pick up a path that will lead you down to the footbridge crossing Hayeswater Gill below the dam. Turn right and follow the rough track down. Hayeswater Gill spills down to Hartsop in some delightful cascades. The building beyond is a Water Board filter-house. As you approach Hartsop the rugged valley of the Pasture Beck opens up to your left, dominated by the rugged profile of Raven Crag. Continue down to the picturesque hamlet of Harstop and subsequently back to your car.

HAWESWATER

Medium/Valley Walk, 11 miles

A Circuit of Haweswater

The sixteen-mile Haweswater Horseshoe, one of the classic Lakeland mountain walks, has no place in a guidebook of this nature. The walk described, however, is a lower-level, shorter, but nonetheless interesting circuit of the reservoir.

Parking: After passing through Bampton, or Bampton Grange, the road to Haweswater passes the turn-off to the hamlet of Burn Banks. Shortly beyond this Naddle Bridge is crossed and where the road bears right is the entrance to Naddle Farm. Park on the grass verge hereabouts. (GR 509157)

WALK up the road to the farm. Go through the farmyard and out of the gate in the top left-hand corner. Do not follow the path up the valley ahead but cross the stile on your left. Cross the Naddle Beck by a ford, next to a covered culvert, and climb the path zig-zagging up through the trees. Leave the trees through a gate and follow a path bearing to the right, with a wall to your left, to reach a further gate. Go through this to step onto a crossing path. Turn right and follow this, keeping a wall to your right. After about a mile this path drops down to a gate. Beyond this gate leave the path and head up to the crest of the hill to your left. Continue along this broad lumpy ridge, Swindale Common, for just over a mile, before dropping down to meet the Old Corpse Road. From the knobbles of Swindale Common there is a glimpse into the lonely valley of Swindale, with the creamy cascades of the Mosedale Beck spilling into the dalehead. Behind is Shap, and its attendant quarries, with the Howgill and Mallerstang fells distantly beyond. Ahead rises the rounded shape of Selside Pike, with Harter Fell beyond, and the domed High Street and shapelier Kidsty Pike to its right. There are no distinct paths on Swindale Common and in thick mist a compass would be essential.

The Old Corpse Road is the Via Doloroso that formerly the Mardale dead made, strapped to pony or sled, to Swindale, and hence to Shap, for burial. A slender guide-post crowns the highest point and a fenced square surrounds a boggy sump that could be the Rowantreethwaite Well marked on the larger O.S. map. Turn right and follow the Corpse Road as it zig-zags down between ruined buildings towards the reservoir. From the steep zig-zag section

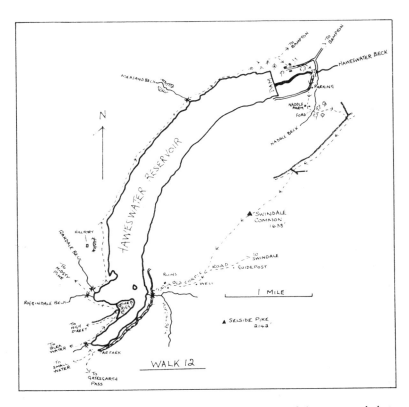

WALK 12

there is a splendid view across the head-waters of the reservoir into the rugged eastern corries of High Street. The Long Stile – Rough Crag ridge, with its wooded foot thrusting out into water, divides Riggindale, on the right, overlooked by Kidsty Pike, from the mountain hollows cupping Blea Water and Small Water. Further left Harter Fell, an amiable-looking fell from most angles, bares the green and grotty crags and gullies of its north-east face.

A gate leads onto the road, which can be followed down to the car-park at its end. The torrid summer of 1984 saw this stretch of the road congested with cars and ice-cream vans as hundreds of 'grockles' poured in to see the ruins of Mardale village revealed by the retreating water. Some attempted to ruin the suspension of their vehicles by vandalising the old pack horse bridge and taking lumps of it home. Alternatively, across the road a gate signposted 'Public Footpath to the Head of the Lake' offers a softer option for the feet.

Go beyond the car-park at the road end shortly to reach a three-fingered signpost near a wall corner. Turn right and follow the sign

'Public Footpath to Bampton'. This goes down, alongside a wall and crossing several boggy patches by duckboards, to a footbridge over the Mardale Beck. Beyond the bridge turn right and follow the path leading out on to the wooded spur, The Rigg, that divides the headwaters of the reservoir. This path presently slants leftwards to reach a wall on the crest of the spur to the left of the trees. On the way ignore paths and a finger-post pointing left; they mark the start of the Rough Crag – Long Stile route to High Street.

Go through a gap in the wall and follow the path down into and around the foot of Riggindale. Sections of this path are lined with upright stones. This is golden eagle country so keep your eyes open. A footbridge of concrete or cement slabs takes you across the Riggindale Beck. Ignore the path beyond heading up the fellside; this leads to Kidsty Pike. Instead bear right shortly to reach and cross a delightful packhorse bridge over cascades of the Randale Beck. Beyond this bridge the path threads through a network of old walls, permanent memorials to the men who once farmed this drowned valley, before passing between a plantation and a wooded promontory. The path then climbs to the summit of Flakehow Crag. On the crest of the crag above and to the left of this high point, Birks Crag, and in a superbly commanding position, are the remains of an Iron Age hill-fort.

This must be one of the most delightful lakeshore paths in Lakeland, if you can shut your eyes to the unnatural 'beach', and forms part of Mr. Wainwright's Coast to Coast Walk. Two miles beyond the hill-fort crag a footbridge crosses the Measand Beck, worth exploring for its splendid rocky gorge, pools and cascades. Shortly after this footbridge trees close off the view of the reservoir, apart from one narrow tree corridor that gives an interesting glimpse of the top of the dam. A mile from the footbridge a stile, with a locked gate to its left, leads into the trees. Cross this and bear leftwards down into the hamlet of Burn Banks. Turn left out of Burn Banks and look for a Coast to Coast sign pointing to a kissing-gate on your right. Beyond this gate follow a path through woods and alongside a beck to reach the road near the Naddle Bridge. Turn right to your car.

The Old Corpse Road,
Swindale and Mosedale Beck Force

An interesting walk over an ancient Via Doloroso and through two of Lakeland's less frequented valleys. It gives a unique mix of varied Lakeland scenery and different aspects of the social and industrial history of Lakeland.

Parking: In the car-park at the Haweswater road-end. (GR 469108).

WALK roughly a mile back up the road where, just beyond the bridge over the Hopgill Beck, you will see a gate on your right signposted 'Old Corpse Road/Swindale'. (This road-walking could be halved by parking in an old quarry half a mile from the road-end). Prior to 1736 the Mardale dead, strapped to sled or pony, were hauled over this path for burial in Shap. Ironically the bones of their descendants suffered a similar fate, being transported to Shap for re-burial when the valley was flooded. The path wends steeply up, passing between the shells of buildings, before the angle eases. From this steep section there is a fine view, across the headwaters of the reservoir, of the rugged eastern flanks of High Street, framed between its acolytes, shapely Kidsty Pike on the right, and bluff, craggy Harter Fell, with the lovely gems of Blea Water and Small Water tucked into its rough contours.

When the angle eases look for a pole on the far skyline indicating your heading and the highest point of the Corpse Road. The path is less distinct across this highest section but odd cairns or upright stones help mark the way. Avoid any faint paths branching left. To your right is a fenced-off sump which could be the Rowantreethwaite Well marked on the large O.S. map. From the pole the view opens up towards Shap, with Mickle Fell peeping over the Pennine rampart beyond. The grassy fell to your immediate right is Selside Pike. I have spotted deer browsing in the combe below it.

The path now descends and shortly meets a wall which it follows down to a beck. Here the wall turns downhill. Cross the beck and follow the path slanting down the fellside towards a lower wall. Turn right and follow this wall down, re-crossing the beck, to a gate. Beyond the gate go down between walls to a lower gate. Beyond this turn right along a track passing a farmhouse and shortly, through gates, to the right of a barn. Continue along a walled lane which eventually emerges into the open, with a dried up tarn bed to its right and the cascades of Mosedale Beck Force away to its left. A

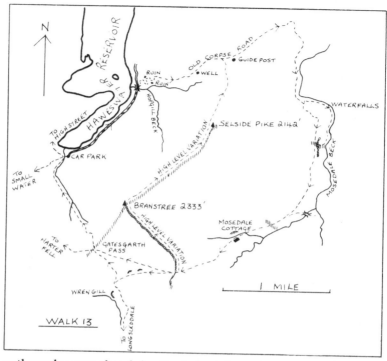

path can be seen ahead slanting leftwards up the shoulder of Selside
Pike. Ignore this and walk left, along the beck, to the foot of the
force.

Now scramble up alongside these fine cascades. Above the falls
continue alongside the beck to reach a fence. Turn right and follow
this uphill to regain the original path where it runs alongside an old
wall. Turn left along this. As this path bears gradually right into
Mosedale it becomes both somewhat indistinct and boggy.
Eventually a footbridge will be seen, below and to your left,
crossing the Mosedale Beck near where it divides. From this bridge
a firmer path heads up Mosedale. Move down to join it. This path
leads to a gate in a fence. After passing through this gate the
abandoned Mosedale Cottage will be seen ahead with extensive old
quarry workings scarring the fellside above it. The path passes to the
right of the cottage. Farmers and shepherds obviously use it for
storage and it appears to have been used as a bothy. A fine, dry one
it is too. Beyond the cottage and its windbreak of trees the path
slants left, then right, around a spur of Branstree, to reach the gate
in the fence crowning the valley head. I've spotted deer several
times around here.

Above and to your right front is Gatesgarth Pass, your next objective, with Harter Fell rising beyond. In front and below is the boggy hollow of Brownhowe Bottom, with the path from Longsleddale to Gatesgarth Pass crossing its far side. Beyond this can be seen the extensive abandoned workings of the Wren Gill Quarry. It appears likely that this quarry is the one referred to in a document of Edward I's reign which contains the earliest recorded reference to a Lakeland quarry.

To reach Gatesgarth Pass either slant directly up and across the fellside towards it, or traverse across the right-hand flank of Brownhowe Bottom, where a faint path links abandoned quarries, to meet the path from Longsleddale. From Gatesgarth Pass a good path leads down to the car-park.

High-level Variation Finish
For those feeling energetic. Turn right at the gate at the head of Mosedale and climb alongside the fence/wall to reach the summit of Branstree. Turn right here and follow a fence for one and a half miles to reach the summit of Selside Pike. Descend due north to meet the Old Corpse Road and return along your outward route.

Walk 14   Fell Walk, 4-5 miles

Small Water, Harter Fell
and Gatesgarth Pass

This must be one of the most enjoyable short mountain walks in Lakeland. The ascent passes through some rugged scenery which is enhanced by a splendid mountain tarn. The descent goes over more amiable ground giving a bird's-eye view of Haweswater.

Parking: As for Walk Thirteen.

LEAVE the car-park shortly to reach a three-fingered signpost near a wall corner. Follow the path directly ahead signposted 'Public Bridleway to Kentmere'. This well-worn path slants gradually upwards under the green and grotty crags and gullies of the north-eastern flank of Harter Fell. It steepens for the final climb to Small Water, crossing a tributary of Small Water Beck by a clapper bridge and then the beck proper by stepping stones where it empties from the tarn.

Small Water, framed between a rugged flank of Harter Fell and the crags of Mardale Ill Bell, which look steep enough to tempt the passing rock-climber, is a gem of a mountain tarn. Here rock and

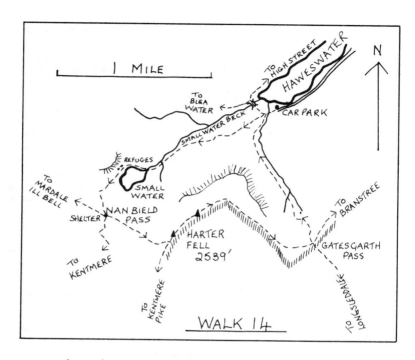

water, the quintessence of Lakeland fell scenery, are sublimely matched. Above and beyond the tarn hangs the rocky notch of Nan Bield Pass, your next objective.

To reach this follow the path around to the right of the tarn and pass across the scree and boulders lying below the crags. The stone structures hereabouts were, according to Mr. Wainwright, shelters built for the protection of travellers overtaken by bad weather when crossing Nan Bield. A final steep climb leads up and into its narrow portals, crowned by a well-constructed windbreak. Beyond and below Kentmere Reservoir nestles in the shadow of a volcano-like Ill Bell. Leftwards, or south-easterly, from Nan Bield a nicely stepped ridge, with just enough rock bursting through to give it a mountain flavour, leads pleasantly to the broad grassy summit of Harter Fell.

The summit cairn incorporates remnants of the old iron boundary fence, giving the appearance of a stand of surrealist weaponry, especially when fronded with ice. The best of the view, for me, is the detailed prospect of the rugged eastern flank of High Street. Deep Blea Water peeps dourly around a flank of Mardale Ill Bell and shapely Kidsty Pike, balanced on its rocky plinth, rises beyond the serrated Long Stile/Rough Crag ridge. Far away to the south-east the hump of Yorkshire's Ingleborough may be picked out.

Just beyond the cairn a wood and wire fence marches across the summit, providing a useful aid to navigation, given bad conditions, all the way down to Gatesgarth Pass. Follow this fence leftwards, north-easterly, and down to a lower, iron-armoured cairn. Beyond this the ground steepens a little before the fence veers abruptly right. Walk to the rocks on the edge here for a superb aerial view of Haweswater Reservoir – a view marred, in my opinion, by the exposed and unnatural beach contour and the added pathos of the lanes and intake walls emerging from the drowned valley.

Bear right and follow the fence down until just above the grassy saddle of Gatesgarth Pass where the path veers away and down to cut a corner. Turn left from the gate crowning the pass and follow the good path back down to the car-park.

Walk 15   Fell Walk, 7 miles

Long Stile, High Street and Kidsty Pike

A friend of mine, whose knowledge of Lakeland is encyclopaedic, claims that the Rough Crag - Long Stile ridge is the finest ridge in Lakeland. I cannot bring myself entirely to agree with him but will go as far as to say that it is the most entertaining way to climb High Street. It is nowhere as slender or airy as the more glamorous 'edges', like Sharp, Striding or Swirrel, but it is longer, and for the peak-bagger has the added bonus of two-thousand footer Rough Crag.

Parking: As for Walks Thirteen and Fourteen.

GO beyond the car-park shortly to reach a three-fingered signpost near a wall corner. Turn right and follow the sign 'Public Footpath To Bampton'. This goes down, alongside a wall and crossing several boggy patches by duckboards, to a footbridge over the Mardale Beck. Beyond the bridge turn right and follow the path leading out onto the wooded spur, The Rigg, that divides the headwaters of the reservoir. This path presently slants up to the left towards the crest of the spur, to the left of the trees. Before reaching the crest a path, indicated by a finger-post, bears left through the bracken. Follow this to meet the wall crowning the crest of the ridge. Turn left, along

43

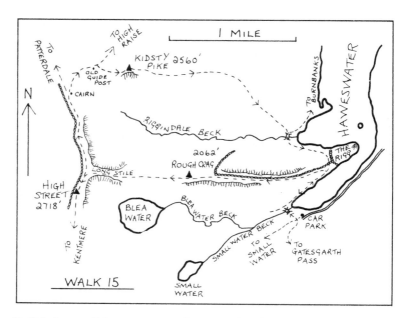

WALK 15

it. It is impossible to go astray because the ridge is well-defined, the Riggindale flank falling away precipitously. The wall turns down into Riggindale just below the summit of Rough Crag.

Beyond Rough Crag the ridge drops down to the grassy saddle of Casper Gate before rearing up again in the slender ridge that is Long Stile proper. Below, to your left, Blea Water, 'the black water', invariably lives up to its name. In the fifties a Brathay Hall exploration group were stunned to record a plummetting depth of over two-hundred feet for this sombre tarn. Long Stile offers no problem in normal conditions but when plastered with snow or ice can become a serious proposition and should not be attempted unless the proper equipment is carried. When the rim of the fell is reached walk south-west across the grass to reach the trig point, and the wall that marches across the fell's broad and grassy dome.

High Street takes its name from the Roman military road that once ran across it, connecting the forts sited near Ambleside and Penrith. Cartographers in the thirteenth century referred to it as 'Brettestreete', or the 'street of the Britons', which suggests this is one of the ancient highways of England. One can see the advantages to our forebears. Well above two thousand feet for much of its length it would be clear of even the highest forest which would mean faster travel and freedom from possible ambush. The Romans would be quick to grasp these advantages, although the thoughts of a raw 'sprog' from the Mediterranean coast sloshing his way across the unprotected summit dome in the teeth of a wet Lakeland spring gale must have been unprintable. The line of the military road shows up best when the mountain is covered in snow. Both from north and south it can be clearly seen climbing across the western shoulder of the summit dome, and late afternoon or evening light highlights its zig-zag descent down the western flank of Froswick into the head of Troutbeck. On the large O.S. map High Street is also christened Racecourse Hill, a relic from the days, prior to 1885, when it was the site of annual shepherds' meets, when strays were handed back to their owners. This was as much a social as a business gathering and horse racing, wrestling and other appropriate Cumbrian junketings went on. The prospect from High Street is wide-ranging but distant, everything close at hand being hidden by the spread of the summit dome. It is from the rims, looking down on Blea Water or Hayes Water, that the most dramatic views are seen.

For the descent head north along the wall eventually to drop down to the saddle at the head of Riggindale. Continue with the wall steeply up the far side until a path branching off to the right, marked with a cairn, is reached. Follow this - it leads around the rim of Riggindale to a cluster of rocks. An old and indecipherable guidepost may be spotted sticking above rocks to your right hereabouts. At this point the Roman Road bears away north-easterly. You continue with the path along the rim, with the drop to your right. This path drops down to a broad grassy saddle before rising up to the airy summit of Kidsty Pike. High Street looks impressive, across the gulf of Riggindale, and through the Straits of Riggindale there's a distant glimpse of the Coniston fells.

A path leads easily down the eastern ridge, climbs over the rocky hiccup of Kidsty Howes, then threads steeply down between rocky outcrops, followed by steep grass, to reach a footbridge of cement slabs over the Riggindale Beck. Cross the bridge and follow the path, often passing between stone uprights, around the lakeshore and up to the crest of The Rigg to meet your outward route.

Four Stones Hill
and Measand Beck

An interesting walk that passes through a mixture of farmland and open fell. Its highlight is the superb view of the gleaming length of Haweswater, and the backcloth of fine fells at its head, from the summit of Four Stones Hill. An ancient enclosure and 'standing stones' close under this summit are a fascinating bonus for those interested in such things.

Parking: Drive over the bridge in Bampton, towards Haweswater. Pass the St. Patrick's Well pub and, about three hundred yards further on, the school. Just past the school, on the left, there is room on the grass verge for about two cars. Otherwise, I'm afraid, it is a matter of finding yourself a space in or around the hamlet, without causing any obstruction. (GR 516178).

WALK back up the road past the school. Look for a gate on your left a few yards to the left of some stone steps. Go through the gate and follow a path slanting leftwards up a field. Soon this path swings right and towards a fence. When the angle eases continue with this fence towards farm buildings ahead, to the left of a plantation. Go through the gate ahead, passing between a wall and a barn, then turn left through a gate. Turn immediately right and follow a wall up a field. Ahead and to your left a stile will be seen climbing a crossing wall. When your wall turns away head for this. Beyond this stile go through a grove of oaks to meet a wall/fence. Turn left and follow this down to a gate in a corner. A glimmer of water away to your left reveals Littlewater Tarn.

Go through the gate to join a path leading out of an adjoining gate and follow it down to a tarmac lane. Turn right up this lane to a junction signposted 'Littlewater Tarn'. Ignore this and continue up the right-hand fork shortly to see a stile on your left. Cross this and go across a field, to the left of a mound crowned by a TV aerial, to reach a stone stile in a wall. Beyond this go leftwards, through more oaks, and down to reach a stone stile in a corner. Cross this and go down, with a wall on your right, towards a dry beck bed. Just before reaching this go through a gate in the wall to your right. Beyond this bear left across the beck bed and climb up into the top left-hand corner of the field, to the left of an imposing barn. In the corner find a stone stile and cross it. Beyond this bear left, to the left of a copse of pine trees, to meet a wall on your right, with a small dilapidated building beyond it. Follow this wall to reach a stone stile in it. Cross

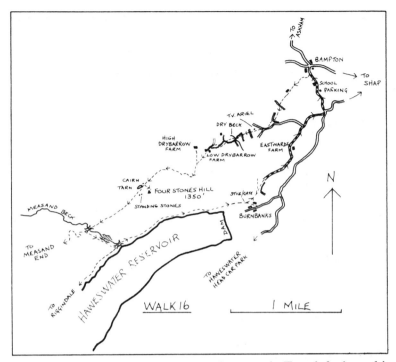

this and head across a field to meet a farm track. Turn left along this and go through a gate into the yard of Low Drybarrow Farm. Go through the yard and to the left of the buildings ahead to pass through a gate and on to the open fell.

Go down into and across a boggy area and up into an obvious gap between two hillocks. You will presently meet a path coming from High Drybarrow Farm. Beyond the gap you get your first glimpse of the head of Haweswater and the fells beyond. The path slants right and down to a boggy beck. Bear left across this, then right again up a slanting path. This swings left and up to meet another boggy beck. Climb either side of this beck, heading up to the right of a rocky hill rising above a dip in the skyline. This is Four Stones Hill, your objective. Beyond the rise you will find an enclosure, marked as an ancient monument on the map, with a small tarn beyond.

From here a short climb leftwards brings you to the summit of Four Stones Hill and a superb view of the gleaming length of the reservoir. Above the steep wooded hills on the far side of the lake rise the rounded shapes of Selside Pike and Branstree, marching rightwards towards the bulkier mass of Harter Fell. To the right of Harter Fell is the knobbly notch of Nan Bield Pass, with the skyline

47

beyond rising towards Mardale Ill Bell. Below and to the right of Nan Bield the fine Rough Crag - Long Stile ridge rises up to the summit of High Street which is hidden by the massive foreground of Measand End, scarred by an old zig-zagging sledgate. To the east, Shap and its quarrries can be seen with the Howgill and Mallerstang fells rising distantly beyond. Further north Crossfell distinctly rears its summit dome over the Eden Valley and the dark uniform rampart of the northern Pennines. The ancient enclosure and the standing stones below the summit of Four Stones Hill, allied to the hill-fort on its Birk's Crag eyrie further up the lake (see Walk Twelve), are all symbols of the past. The drowned valley and the ruddy rampart of the dam are all symbols of the present. Only the dark crumpled fells are timeless. Given certain conditions of light and weather these factors add a sense of mystery to this view.

Return down to the enclosure and go past the tarn. Just beyond it you will see, on your left, the 'standing stones'. Continue down a path through the bracken, passing above and to the right of a plantation, and heading towards the bulk of Measand End, to reach the footbridge over the Measand Beck. Beyond the bridge turn immediately left and follow a footpath leading down the right bank of the beck to a junction with the lakeshore path near a footbridge. The Measand Beck is delightful, and well worth exploring, running through a fine rocky gorge and spilling into alternately delightful cascades and pools. A fine place to snooze by or plunge into, given the right weather of course.

Cross the footbridge and follow the lakeshore path back towards the foot of the reservoir. Eventually woods hide the water although there is a glimpse down a narrow tree corridor of the crest of the dam. Just over a mile after leaving the Measand Beck a stile, with a locked gate to its left, offers access into the woods. Take the path bearing leftwards, away from the stile. When this forks take the left-hand path shortly to meet a wall. Follow this to a gate leading into a walled lane. Follow this lane - later the right wall falls away – through several gates to reach Eastward Farm. Pass through two gates to the left of the farm to reach a farm road. Follow this down to a lower road which is then followed down to a junction. Turn left to reach your car.

Warning: The lane mentioned above is not designated a public right-of-way. In answer to my inquiries the farmer at Eastward said walkers used it regularly and he had no objection to them using it as long as they remembered to shut gates. If, however, in the future you should find sign declaring this 'private', or the farmer objects to your presence, do not quote this book as your authority to pass that way. In such a case return to the stile, cross it and go down into the hamlet of Burnbanks. Turn left here to meet the road where a left turn and just over a mile of road-walking will see you back at your car.